LOVE, LAUGHS, AND LEARNING

LOVE, LAUGHS, AND LEARNING

Humorous Tales from the Classroom

AVERY NIGHTINGALE

Creative Quill Press

CONTENTS

1	Introduction	1
2	The Power of Humor in Education	3
3	Funny Classroom Moments	4
4	Lessons Learned Through Laughter	6
5	The Role of Teachers in Creating a Lighthearted Environment	8
6	Using Humor to Enhance Learning	10
7	Building Connections Through Comedy	12
8	Benefits of Incorporating Humor in Education	14
9	Overcoming Challenges with a Smile	16
10	The Impact of Humor on Student Engagement	18
11	Encouraging Creativity and Critical Thinking with Humor	19
12	Fostering a Positive Classroom Culture through Laughter	21
13	The Psychology of Laughter and Learning	23
14	Strategies for Implementing Humor in Teaching	25
15	The Role of Laughter in Classroom Management	27
16	Inspiring Confidence and Resilience through Humor	29

CONTENTS

17	Using Jokes and Puns to Reinforce Concepts	31
18	Incorporating Funny Stories and Anecdotes in Lessons	32
19	The Art of Timing and Delivery in Humorous Teaching	34
20	The Benefits of Humor for Teacher-Student Relationships	36
21	Creating Memorable Learning Experiences with Humor	38
22	The Role of Laughter in Reducing Stress and Anxiety	40
23	Using Humor to Address Sensitive Topics and Difficult Subjects	42
24	Balancing Humor and Professionalism in the Classroom	44
25	Incorporating Humor in Different Subjects and Grade Levels	46
26	The Impact of Humor on Academic Performance	48
27	Strategies for Engaging Shy and Introverted Students through Humor	50
28	The Role of Improvisation and Spontaneity in Humorous Teaching	52
29	Encouraging Collaboration and Teamwork through Humor	54
30	The Connection between Humor and Emotional Intelligence	56
31	Using Humor as a Tool for Classroom Management	58
32	Conclusion	60

Copyright © 2024 by Avery Nightingale

All rights reserved. No part of this book may be reproduced in any manner whatsoever without written permission except in the case of brief quotations embodied in critical articles and reviews.

First Printing, 2024

CHAPTER 1

Introduction

The tales are divided into eleven parts, or "Periods," each of which covers a different aspect of teaching. For example, Period 1 deals with teaching, Period 2 is about learning, and Period 8 is about electronics in the classroom. The stories may be used as delightful diversions for anyone who has taught or can remember students. A secondary audience will recognize challenging situations faced by institutions during a period of rapid change in educational methods and technologies, and the use of humor as a coping mechanism. I tried to be as truthful as possible when retelling the events described in these stories. I even changed the names of the characters when the anecdotes involved some type of tragedy; all other aspects are accurate. It is my hope that college professors who mentor pre-service teachers, reading specialists, and colleagues whose backgrounds are in the classroom and/or communications and education disciplines, will have experienced similar events. Enjoy the stories and participate in our laughter.

Most teachers spend their entire careers collecting humorous tales from their classrooms. I have only been teaching for eight years, and my "Funny File" is bursting at the seams. My college professors emphasized the need to show students that learning could be fun. I laughed in agreement, but as a teacher, I have found that my attempts at "fun learning" often opened the door for the unexpected. I am now writing about some of these events.

CHAPTER 2

The Power of Humor in Education

It is also important for students to reduce anxiety and gain confidence. Positive attitudes result in better learning outcomes. have separately pointed out that the best teaching skill is to create humorous situations. The most supportive person in recent years is Kooshan Poursoltan, a physics teacher, a mother, and a natural stand-up comedian at the Physics department of San Francisco State University. Coşkun and Oluk (2010) envision the necessity of humor in education and claim that both students and teachers appreciate and practice humorous situations with similar skill, but when excessive force is directed towards the teacher, the appreciation level of both declines."

"In 'The Power of Humor in Education,' Jolly (2004) states that humorous situations can catch the attention of students, help them remember knowledge by connecting it with funny images easily, and avoid the affective filters that make learning difficult. Humor is an important learning tool and is essential to any subject. Nobel laureate Arthur Schawlow at Princeton University humorously asserts, 'you can't broadcast pictures of a white horse on a white wall' (details in Palmer, 2003). Humor can deliver information in diversified modalities, aiming at the students.

CHAPTER 3

Funny Classroom Moments

These misunderstandings don't only happen in science, they can happen in math as well. In a first-grade math class, my teacher professor had instructed me to teach my students the concept of equal groups. I asked my students to illustrate this idea by drawing four groups. The resulting pictures caused fits of laughter. "Now, what's in each group?" I asked a cute little student named Henry. Proudly he stood and said, "I have three people in my first group; Maria has four trees in her group; Jenny has two oceans; and Jimmy drew two buildings in his!" I thanked each child for their wonderful illustrations and began a discourse on how each group should be similar. Three mimes of my explanation later, the students realized their errors, and laughing, corrected their pictures.

I often have students that hail from different countries and so English is not their native language. Sometimes this leads to humorous occurrences. For example, I was teaching my students the days of the week and their unique spellings. "Monday begins with em," I said. "Tuesday begins with tee." A kindergartner named Mari quickly corrected me. "Tee? No! Tuesday begins with choo." I later learned that the word in her country, Bulgaria, for Tuesday - вторник - sounds like choosday, so she had made an honest mistake.

4

Students, especially younger ones, often misunderstand sound words. So, when I read a children's story about cows, my six-year-old students looked at me questioningly as I read the words, "The cows go moo." I was amazed when I learned that they thought it was the cows that said "Moo?" One little girl saved the day, however, when she quickly corrected her peers. "No, the moo goes cow," she said with assurance. Not wanting to spoil the moment with a grammar lesson, I let the matter drop.

CHAPTER 4

Lessons Learned Through Laughter

For Lydia, my profoundly cerebral, though directionally challenged sixth-grader, learning came slowly and with great effort. The journey that is her thought process took several jaunts toward the center of enlightenment. Although Lydia topped each arduous ascent with the stage presence of the bookworm she is, she usually left her humor area —also known as the polis by most country-folk—masked from visiting onlookers. Small giggles muttered jadedly beneath peach-fuzzy chins were quite harmless, if inconspicuous. Usually, Lydia's ostentatious bravo comedy would erupt during the dull moments when the teacher revealed nothing new, or when I revealed too much. Instances demanding intellectual agility from poor Lydia triggered the unfortunate Sprague response too often to be seasonal misuse. One such outburst began when, one crisp, November day, I questioned, "Now, I want everyone to remember to put the least common denominator into every math problem before adding or subtracting anything, multiplicatively or linearly."

I first entered Stephen F. Austin State University's Department of Human Services as an enthusiastic, twenty-two-year-old young man with no practical knowledge of what school is all about. After finishing my usual first-day speech, I began writing my name on the board. It was the first time the students would see my full surname, which is Fletcher. I had no idea what I was in for when, between my first two consonants, a shrill, slender voice called out, "Hey, what are you, a wolf or something?" I turned around to see who was being so disrespectful, and little Freddy Ford from the corner of my eye caught my attention. He sat in his chair, with a toothy grin and a face that "wasn't" that innocent for a young, blonde-haired, blue-eyed third-grader. I gave him "the look" that Mrs. Clarkson said teachers are born with, and then I wondered how often people call my kin "wolves." Dearly I regret not pestering my thinly-blonde, boyishly-primitive cousins with their third-grade, wolf-related jibes the previous holidays, as I could have seen then how black "poor Freddy's teeths was."

CHAPTER 5

The Role of Teachers in Creating a Lighthearted Environment

The classroom is a great place to introduce and practice the value of humor in other areas of life. A college student now realizes how important humor is in his adult life and future career, and plans to use even more humor as a teacher himself. He argues, "Teachers who use humor in their teaching leave a lasting and creative imprint on us as well as on the world of education". One must learn what and how to laugh at specific times in numerous situations which may include adult and child events, as well with a variety of people. The positive attitude, ease, and generous nature lights the path to success, and makes our future professional lives and personal lives less stressful, more memorable and wonderful.

Although the literature has not quantified this prescriptive stance, many authors and scholars believe that as humor is good for both children and adults, it should be included in the classroom. The issue is whether teachers should work harder to include more humor. Teachers who incorporate humor education like humor use in the classroom, send the message to their students that "humor is healthy, and is very important in creating a lighthearted environment. Children and adults who are in a classroom that periodically witnesses the teacher performing humorous activities are more likely to be practicing humor by the same individuals. Creating a lighthearted environment in the classroom leads to class rapport of appreciation for the value of humor. Additionally, teachers who use humor in their instructional classrooms have been found to have students who show "increased attention to task, improved retention and learning of information, and heightened performance, motivation and class interest created respectful classroom environments, positive class ethos, and generally effective educators.

CHAPTER 6

Using Humor to Enhance Learning

Learning can be maximized by utilizing both formal (i.e., pre-planned) and informal (i.e., spontaneous) types of humor in the classroom. Informal humor—also known as spontaneous or reactive humor—results primarily from off-the-cuff remarks that instructors make, in an attempt to make learning social. Instructors may use spontaneous humor to create a lighthearted atmosphere, which can generate a sense of social recognition and facilitate classroom bonding. A warm, well-organized classroom is likely to encourage a variety of comments and a relaxed environment. This student-teacher interaction emphasizes a joint task, focusing student motivation and increasing the likelihood for student success. Informal humor can reflect and create a relaxed social environment, fostering a close attachment between instructors and students. Of all types of humor, informal humor may be the most ideal type of humor for educators to incorporate into their classroom, as classroom humor sessions with predetermined material may actually increase student anxiety rather than reducing stress in the classroom.

More and more research and anecdotal evidence indicates that humor can enhance student learning. Both undergraduates and college students have noted improvement in achievement, class attention, learning motivation, and students' likelihood to read and complete assignments when humor is used in the classroom. When humor is used during instruction, students are more likely to report that they are excited and enjoy learning. Students may also experience less nervousness and less frustration completing their assignments and taking tests. Additionally, students are more likely to report increased self-esteem and self-confidence completing challenging assignments and performing classroom-related activities.

CHAPTER 7

Building Connections Through Comedy

Laughter may be a universal experience, but jokes are subtle. They rely on very specific shared knowledge and contextual clues in order to succeed. From idioms to stereotypes and shared experiences, jokes primarily rely on the safety of shared experience in order for the punch line to connect to the audience. Therefore, while humor may bring us together, it is through the subtlety of jokes that we build relationships with those whom we share the experiences. When jokes miss the mark for some of the audience, they reinforce the concept of being an outsider instead of an insider because those who are "in the know" share a belief that sets them apart and makes them the butt of the joke. In the classroom, one of the goals is to build a community of learners. Often, in college and technical classrooms, students are divided into two main groups. The first, residential students (RS) live in the halls and on campus. The other group is made up of non-residential students (NRS), who typically are over 24 and often have work or family obligations. How then can one use humor to bring these diverse groups of students together?

When you watch Jerry Seinfeld or attend an improv group's performance at a comedy club, their jokes may include familiar observations about life, human nature, and everyday occurrences. As they tell their stories, the audience peers back into their own familiar experiences and finds reflection and enjoyment in the universal laughs of the everyday. Laughter, then, can be a bridge that builds connections as people recognize life's experiences that we share throughout our society. This universal recognition, however, is not where relationships are built.

CHAPTER 8

Benefits of Incorporating Humor in Education

Teachers turning to humor in the classroom often exhibit a high sense of self-efficacy. They believe in their abilities to handle the class. This inevitably portrays an air of confidence, which impacts teacher learning and student learning. Also, a teacher who is not in an anxious state can more easily focus on student needs and respond positively. Managing a classroom is no easy task. Use of humor makes the heavy task seem lighter and more manageable. When students enjoy the process of learning they are likely to retain information for a longer period. There are lots of ways to use humor in the university classroom, such as: icebreakers, jokes, puns, cartoons, skits, and music. Whatever the means, if used appropriately and effectively, mixing humor with imagination paves the way for more meaningful learning, because humor helps people to remember better. It acts like a hook, connecting the unfamiliar territory of new knowledge with something known, familiar, and comfortable, making the journey to understanding more tolerable and enjoyable.

A major benefit of humor is that it immediately captures attention. Imagine a lecturer beginning a lecture on a dull note by stating, "So we will be discussing vascular diseases today" or "Today we will be discussing the American Civil War." Many students will start pulling out and fiddling with their smartphones. Throw in a wisecrack—and voilà, everyone's attention is fixed on you. The lecturer has managed to conquer the competitors for the students' attention for at least the next few minutes. Once you manage to capture the students' attention, engaging them becomes easier. Humor often lightens the mood in the classroom. Students, more so the shy ones, tend to be more communicative and open in classrooms where humor plays an integral role. This is due to the classroom being perceived as an amiable gathering rather than a serious den where all sorts of unnatural requests, demands, and expectations are imposed. The resultant openness tends to lay a setting that is conducive to learning.

Some of the benefits of incorporating humor in education are outlined below.

CHAPTER 9

Overcoming Challenges with a Smile

Love, Laughs, and Learning: Humorous Tales from the Classroom tells humorous teaching stories and gives solid, practical advice to first-time teachers. Ms. DeGray's work is especially useful to those who are looking for light-hearted material about classroom experiences. My goal for next month is to have the jokes be just as humorous, but to be on me. A little "you'll never guess what DeGray did today" camaraderie will strengthen student relationships and involve them in a game that focuses on behaviors that build trust and relationships. I will keep their trust, as well as control, with laughter. I'm teaching a year full of mirth and creating an environment where students mirror my efforts, learn, and succeed.

During my first year of teaching, I wanted to be seen as a knowledgeable instructor and the person they loved to see each day. I felt like a failure since I couldn't control them the way they held in check in my observation class. The crazy mathematicians handed me a tissue and sent me to the lavatory or helped explain things to the boisterous students taking the equation apart as I led demonstrations. They were my friends and we worked as a team to give each other our best. I taught diligently while risking their respectful tolerance with frequent quizzes and tests. I sopped up IV drips of praise to condition their behavior and mixed in a coagulate of amusement.

My first year in teaching left me mentally, physically, and emotionally drained. In June, rallied by the support of my husband and the school staff, I returned to work, ready to prove that I could control my students, keep their fatigue to a minimum, keep my classroom in line, and reflect progress on their standardized tests. The students apparently understood my needs and gleefully cooperated by leaving me written solutions to Equations of the Day such as, "Let x be driving age. Assume the car is going 60 mph. Solve for the degree of the tears on Ms. DeGray Owl's face as she drives home." Their zingers brightened my day and showed me that laughter can melt the biggest crisis into a mild annoyance.

CHAPTER 10

The Impact of Humor on Student Engagement

Alfonso formed two groups by dividing her students into two different classes. One class was then exposed to the same humorous lighthearted comments that they had been exposed to throughout the entire course, and the other was not. The accumulation of the scores (Homework 30%, Midterm Exam 20%, The Final Exam 40%, Participation (Attendance & Quizzes in the classroom) 10%) tested only as described in the syllabus, and never by being asked to memorize a definition or name. Alfonso found that, for the purpose of this formative research, the uninformed control group fared significantly worse throughout the semester.

In this writing, we'll continue with our study of how humor impacts the learning process. Being curious about whether humor increased student grades or not, Stephanie R. Alfonso, instructor of French at the University of South Florida in Tampa, conducted this experiment. She began to suspect that humorous comments boosted student comprehension and memory while monitoring her own speech, as well as that of other successful and engaging lecturers and professors, during the course of her teaching. The purpose of the experiment was to ascertain whether or not using humor while teaching college students improved students' academic achievement in terms of grades.

CHAPTER 11

Encouraging Creativity and Critical Thinking with Humor

Second, this small act exemplifies an objective to which teachers in public speaking, as well as in any communication discipline, should strive. This objective—a critical thinking objective—concerns itself with (a) devising different ways to think about/topics and (b) letting students know about (a). According to Paul and Elder (2008), understanding entails better thinking. When students gain a better understanding, a better communication product should be the result. If teaching in public speaking means something more meaningful than simply providing simple strategies for combative strategies, (a) and (b) is especially helpful to developing good public speaking skills. Paul and Elder detail thirty-five key principles to which all Disciplines should attend when developing our instruction in an attempt to make students who are deeply learned. There research only helps fulfill the strategic objective that is public speaking's raison d'etre.

The first paragraph is to welcome future students to the course and provide information needed to ensure that the atmosphere is immediately established. Telling a joke in what is sometimes thought of as public speaking (an introductory lecture) that also emphasizes what I hope students will see as my main objective always guarantees ear-to-ear grins. No longer is my relationship with uneasy, apprehensive, tired, hungry, busy students an arcane mystery. Teachers have found that, (a) when students laugh together, the atmosphere is more relaxed, (b) a levity can often defuse tension which may have developed from coercion (such as from the teacher himself) (Kauffman, Ryan, & Ferguson, 1983), (c) students will laugh and engage—having students go into stressless chuckles because of something the Graduate Teaching Assistant (GTA) has said is one of our most attainable rewards.

CHAPTER 12

Fostering a Positive Classroom Culture through Laughter

People often suggest that if any part of the lesson could be made "fun", it is important to integrate "fun" into the learning environment. From a young age, humans are naturally playful. Indeed, the freedom of children to play is recognized as a basic human right by the United Nations. The impulse to laugh and express joy is merely a fraction compared to the laughter shared after a mutual understanding or unity. The reason students and teachers are so fond of laughter in the classroom is not simply laughing at jokes, but demonstrates that humor is an influential tool in establishing connections between people. When teachers and students have a connection beyond content knowledge, the content knowledge is better transferred and content knowledge is continuously acquired.

A typical day in a classroom is filled with routine matters, such as how to write the letter "r" properly, the concept of a distributive property, or formation of the past tense. Nevertheless, exceptional moments, like a big laugh or two, would be remembered forever. Sometimes the big laughter erupts when the teacher has just casually shared a short, unprepared story or has gone off track with a joke during a math explanation.

When I have visitors in my classroom, they often say that my lessons are "fun". I usually laugh at this statement, because what may appear to be "fun" or easily prepared is the result of hours of preparation and reflection focusing on what makes sense to share with my students.

CHAPTER 13

The Psychology of Laughter and Learning

I'll probably never be happy with the answers to the question of: 'Why laugh?', but I think we can all agree that having a good laugh in class, a class where a professor-pitchman can seize the opportunities presented by humor to engage students in their education, is the ultimate secret ingredient to laughter and learning.

As adults, we laugh 10-100 times a day, making up 10-15% of our daily conversation. Yet, we laugh significantly less in adulthood than childhood. Infants have been known to laugh 300 times a day. Why fewer laughs in adulthood? Laughter is a part of the human system – just like we require food or sleep; we also require laughter. However, as with eating and sleeping, many adults find ways to put off something so basic and healthy. Also, we're usually not even aware of the magic of laughter and how important it is to just feeling good and functioning well. We take it for granted, but just try going a day without laughing. And yet, even employees laugh much less in the presence of a supervisor or someone of higher status (which may explain why Stephen Colbert's better half stayed off camera in the classroom). As if life isn't already too scary, there are actually doctors who specialize in the science of laughter called gelotologists – and, Dr. Lee S. Berk and his research partner Dr. Stanley Tan have found that laughter turns on genes that are essential for healing and inhibits genes that code for proteins implicated in stress and inflammation.

One of the great mysteries I hope to address in my work and my book is just why is humor so important and so under-utilized? Maybe one reason laughter is not more prevalent in the university classroom is because it seems 'un-professorial'. A course on the psychology of humor in higher education may also have the added bonus of helping professors realize that laughter in class is not frivolous; laughter is fundamental to who we are and therefore, integral to our educational development.

CHAPTER 14

Strategies for Implementing Humor in Teaching

What I now prefer to do is plan for the unexpected in my teaching methods. Instead of doing something the same way I have always done it, I try to be as surprised as the students will be. I believe that good teaching must be both critical and engaging. The goal is not just to share knowledge but also to inspire students to think a little differently or at least keep them from having a total meltdown at the end of the week. Doing something new and surprising is an enigma in the world of teaching. Even the word enigma is humorous, offering a bit of play on words with the word "frustration" by taking pieces of key information and pulling it back together in a fresh, new way.

Humor can be an effective tool in teaching and learning, and yet it remains one of the most underused and undervalued. Instructors easily become too fixed in their formulas, easy answers, and tradition. True learning and positive change happen in the confluence of fun, surprise, and discord. It is important to find the good amid the bad, wet among dry. Humor adds the "wet" to our teaching—making our students wake up, think a little harder, and hopefully come away with valuable critical thinking skills. As hard as humor is to sell in teaching, what's important is that, to the degree possible, we take the time to search beyond the expected and underneath the traditional for ways to wake up, surprise, and challenge our students.

CHAPTER 15

The Role of Laughter in Classroom Management

Teachers often think their students don't laugh. We would, on average, expect students to respond to teacher humor every forty-five to ninety seconds. If not at least smiling, teachers should question whether they have become disconnected or detached from their students. If laughter is present, then, as Hamre, Pianta, and Chazen-Cohen stated, the classroom appears to be relationship-rich. Laughter may not grow or nurture relationships, but it does indicate they are already healthy. In classrooms where students appear to be relational, they are also most likely to rate their teachers as successful at preventing and resolving conflicts. If laughter provides no additional benefits, it at least suggests a certain state of the class.

The role of laughter in classroom management: Adolescents are often challenged in a number of ways, not the least of which is their interactions with their classmates and their unfolding judgment of themselves. Humor provides a rest from self-absorption and diffuses tension when things don't go according to plan. When adolescents were asked what they most remembered of their teacher's routines, the most popular responses were made-up songs, sound effects, and jokes, and that this then eases the impact of corrective feedback on learning. Comer and Bueschel categorized teacher humor into five types: supply humor that involves handing something to the students and acting as though they already have it; benign violation that breaks a norm but is not malicious; incongruity that poses a puzzle or absurd situation; resolution humor that works out, in a way students did not expect, a dilemma; and playfulness that includes high levels of energy and sudden movements.

CHAPTER 16

Inspiring Confidence and Resilience through Humor

The teacher had arranged practices in responding poetically to words spoken, and as a result of a deal that she and her students struck before the previous poem was read, for reciting this blue-eyed slave, Billy got to scribble in the dirt. As Williams, just before his clinical note about Brady's bradycardia or slow pulse, parenthetically expressed a dire warning followed by a comma after the passage about the brave sparrow, Miss Pritch sensed the importance of that particular phrase and emphasized it by pausing, despite the students' anticipation of what extraordinary offering they could expect from Billy. While communicating to Mrs. Pritchard, formerly known as Miss Pritch, Billy revealed the significance of the scheme in empathetic poetry readings, authored under the names of fellow students who must have expressed prior to this special literary blooming. In front of the rediscovered original voice and his peers, Billy won, awe-struck by Miss Pritch's first name, budding empowerment.

In "Brave Sparrow," Virginia Owens portrayed a young boy named Billy who was respected and liked, but whom everyone perceived as being somewhat odd. Billy possessed a doctorate in elementary psychology and "scorned the idea of common sense." Despite his peculiarities, which would be enough to bother any child, except of course Billy, the nine-year-old emanated an attitude of self-confidence that hid any vulnerability. His white teacher, an elderly, wise, and astute woman, overhearing comments about Billy's unusual response to an insensitive, cruel, and inappropriate attack from the back of the room, which Billy "deflected with a learned comprehension that refused to shield itself or the boys who attacked him," was moved to tears. Sometime later, during an arithmetic lesson, the teacher, Mrs. Pritchard, or Miss Pritch as she was affectionately called by her students, broke the imposed class rules by reading aloud from the beauty. Long, wild, and yellow, it was the poem that gave the book its title. The poem described a brave sparrow whose wings were cropped. The bird overcame dullness, a flightless spirit, and cruel teasing to soar far above the oppressors who grounded it.

CHAPTER 17

Using Jokes and Puns to Reinforce Concepts

In discussing Zeeman effects, I stated that classroom lights affected atomic behavior. At the next class, I placed a small refrigerator near the lectern, ran an orange extension cord through the door, stood the door about one fourth open, and maintained a stack of files close to the compartment. I referred to that "frigography" to demonstrate radiations and comment that the refrigerator was what remained of my jokes. If students are not interested in the serious aspects of your subject, they will still be interested in puns. When possible, use humor in introductions, summaries, and reviews. Tell light jokes followed by some serious thoughts: "Some of you may be startled when I tell you that bubbles are 'amoebas of our thoughts.' You will be even more startled when I then say that amoebas are models of our body's problem solvers."

Jokes and puns are effective teaching tools for reinforcing concepts. Whenever you can insert puns or jokes into your lectures, do so. For example, in teaching the principles of refrigeration and the use of refrigerants, insert this early into your lecture: "Before we go on, I want to tell you that five sixths of the earth's population believe refrigerants are liquids, and the other one-sixth are puzzled."

CHAPTER 18

Incorporating Funny Stories and Anecdotes in Lessons

To adapt this story for a presentation, teachers can get small ships from the stationary store and pour some water with a little flour to make it cloudy. This will make the students curious to find out what the ships look like when they entered the canal. And to make it a little related, we can connect and present the story of how our ancestors in the early times used canals to travel during the olden times and adapt the stories of their travels. While retelling the story, the teacher could point out at various places, while the student can fill the relative landmarks they would come across during their journey through the canal is a big part of the learning that we do in the classrooms. On the net, this is all what is left for posterity in a changing world. By pictures, drawings, etc. And the student would remember this disciplining story, as sun, wind, and water are the great motivators and we learn by using our natural senses. This would also show that lesson planning has to begin right from the day you give the introduction, and not the last minute preparation.

Funny stories and anecdotes can be used to connect to a lesson or topic and make learning a little bit more fun. There is a popular story that tells us the importance of preparing from the start. It tells us that the trainer advised 2 participants to be present at the same time and told them that they needed to prepare a presentation for the next day. The seller from the south meeting the buyer from the north. So, everyone did their assignment and the first participant shared his favorite of the vintage ship traveling through the Suez Canal, making the presentation vivid and engaging. The ship was hitting the canal walls, people were having a great time. One person apparently asked how old the ship was and the reply from the participant was "3 Years" and the other person asked what brand of paint they were using. And he replied his ship. The buyer from the north was very keen and made a purchase. The trainer then asked the other participant who was from the north, "Can you make the required presentation?" And the participant replied with a presentation "About the Ship with 3 holes".

CHAPTER 19

The Art of Timing and Delivery in Humorous Teaching

What I have learned, however, is that I can teach comedy timing and delivery strategies that can help colleges of education students pair humor with serious teaching content and get their students to relax and laugh while they are learning. Sometimes students take a course on Effective Instruction in the Content Areas, and they think they will be able to demonstrate their understanding of the content area by performing the way my daddy did. The students think they will enjoy the class in the same way they enjoyed my father's class, but this is not always the case. My confidence has taken a serious hit because, as I have worked to cultivate my comedic timing and delivery, I've felt less funny than I've ever felt in my life. But my daddy showers me with praise, reminding me that for many of his years I was and continue to be his muse.

My daddy was a college and high school teacher and a stand-up comedian, and he kept his students in stitches throughout the course of his teaching career. In large part because of him, I am pursuing a career in education and want to follow in his humorous teaching footsteps. It has been a challenge for me to begin to master his comedic timing and delivery. My students tell me that I'm funny, but I feel that I'm a long way from reaching the level at which my daddy performed. My daddy did not just tell jokes, he turned his entire class period into a stand-up act. I have never met anyone as gifted at teaching with humor as my dad was. I am in awe of his teaching abilities.

CHAPTER 20

The Benefits of Humor for Teacher-Student Relationships

A teacher engaging in laughter relates directly to the relational dimension. Through this laughter, the teacher is humanized. Too often, teacher-student relationships are defined by power relations, with a regular display of laughter a marker of the more powerful. When teachers are seen laughing (and laughing with), they share the quality of frailty that is inherent in all human beings; they become more human in the eyes of the students. Simply put – the act of laughter can effect increased liking other human beings. Through laughter, individuals are more positively perceived. The reason for this might be laughter brings joy and relaxation to people, thereby increasing attractiveness. When teachers laugh at student jokes, they perceive the teacher as warmer. Laughter also acknowledges disclosure; in sharing laughter with the student, teachers are confirming and encouraging the share. A supportive climate is thereby created – one that has been shown to augment student academic and socio-emotional life.

There are many reasons to use humor in teaching. The most obvious benefit is that humor adds merriment temporarily to life. However, several additional and often overlooked advantages can result from the use of instructional humor. It can increase student motivation, attention, and retention. Laughter takes the drudgery out of learning and allows lessons to be enjoyable and interesting. It stimulates the mind and can lead to greater critical understanding. Comedy can also startle by presenting information in slightly different ways and opening new perspectives. Instructional humor can decrease student anxiety and defuse tension that may be present in the classroom. Most importantly, it makes the teacher more human and approachable.

CHAPTER 21

Creating Memorable Learning Experiences with Humor

In a mere 14 weeks, I was not only the favorite professor of all 27 adults, but I held claim on the best seating and decor to maintain if a barricade system was ever necessary. Professors of the new bilingual preschool classroom consistently commented on the high spirits, respect for one another, and the obvious camaraderie in room 205. They would place me right up there with the wise old owl mascot calling the shots from right in the middle of the peacekeeping "back row" if it were not for the flyers stating that the Presidential Election was not a jelly wrestling tournament. Since I offered them a send-off that ended with them executing more cartwheels than instructions for launching the Swedish Corpse Launcher, I suggested we start calling ourselves Profesora's Comando.

On the other hand, there have been times when I have created very memorable learning experiences by introducing humor to my students for the first time. For example, one of my most memorable classes was a group of 20-somethings I taught Spanish I to for the first time. As mentioned in Chapter 6, they adored their Spanish-speaking professor and loudly greeted me with "¡Hola Profesora!" after every break. I truly enjoyed turning in and reading their exams because of their back page, or new word of the day, where all 27 students always remembered to write a new Spanish word on their consistently blank back page, and always raved about which word they had chosen at the start of the subsequent class period. At their request, I would ham it up, then give them clues when we were five or fewer minutes early to enter inquiries for the day on vocabulary they could use in their daily lives.

The use of humor in the classroom can increase learning, make students more open to being educated, and make you, as an educator, more memorable. While there are a few general tips for adding humor to your curriculum, such as not offending anyone or avoiding making kids feel uncomfortable, experienced educators agree that most humorous stories about interacting with the students and/or observing them in the classroom usually come up during the second or subsequent years. I would have to agree.

CHAPTER 22

The Role of Laughter in Reducing Stress and Anxiety

One of the most effective forms of stress relief that humor offers is its ability to decrease a person's ranger to experience fear. Recounting humorous scenarios experienced in the classroom on any rainbow spectrum – from entertainingly abnormal to endearing – serves as a crucial reservoir of laughter that deescalates stress. In considering how fear dilutes stress resilience, Lavretsky offers a comprehensive review of the role of chronic fear in elevating inflammatory markers, thereby compromising an individual's stress response. In biological terms, these stress deescalators are driven with laughter's capacity to raise beta-endorphins while simultaneously regulating cortisol, thus restoring a sense of humor-mediated well-being. This humor-induced well-being has proven to mitigate amygdala hyperactivity. More significant to the classroom however is laughter's ability to suppress subjectively perceived stress, recognize unregulated levels of depressive symptoms and inflammatory markers.

Many an insightful, life-changing conversation occurs between family members, friends, peers, and mentors over the sharing of humor, and it is within this spirit that we highlight lighthearted, anecdotal stories of educational relations. For example, humor has been explored as a means to enrich student learning, thus this discourse meets the pedagogical aim of fostering collegial humor rituals, or shifts in culture to mold a positive, humor-rich learning environment that unlocks genuine participation and learning. Furthermore, our working goal as serving (or preparing to be) educators is to keep a pulse on our own stress and cultivate the humility to laugh at what is difficult. Hollis has reflected on laughter as "emotional self-soothing" which results in "fuller lives" in accord with traditional bathroom humor. Thus, we provide pedagogical insight to reduce feelings of teacher isolation and enhance interactions through recorded laughter resonance.

CHAPTER 23

Using Humor to Address Sensitive Topics and Difficult Subjects

Using humor in the classroom can even help the teacher address sensitive or difficult classroom topics. One study explored this by examining how humor was used in three different history courses on the topic of the Vietnam War. It indicated that instructors that used humor interacted with students differently, and how these two classroom environments came to influence student learning and understanding in unique ways. Instructors in the two classes that used humor were more effective at addressing potentially distressing subjects, offering neutrality to support more open debates, and enhanced learning by asking open-ended questions and incorporating students' previous experiences. Students also expressed experiencing less stress in classes where humorous comments were employed. Moreover, students in these courses were more likely to discuss the war with family and friends outside of the classroom, a finding that underscores how the instructors' perception had a positive effect on their absorption and retention of knowledge commented in class.

Other research has demonstrated that instruction that elicits genuine laughter, or is perceived as humorous, results in better learning outcomes. In a study by Sun (2012), participants who had been instructed using a course that incorporated a significant level of humor perceived the videos as more interesting and less boring. The instructor was rated as more confident and more understanding. Moreover, the instructor was ranked as doing a better job presenting the learning materials and fostering a learning environment, leading participants to express a stronger motivation to enroll in other courses with the instructor that used humor. Similarly, Robert and Yan (2007) found that lecture content that included humor was associated with higher student engagement and with a positive impact on students' perception of how effective the teacher was at enabling learning.

CHAPTER 24

Balancing Humor and Professionalism in the Classroom

As teachers who've chosen to teach the four most hilarious years in education, it behooves us to stay off the plain road, and veer ever so slightly off the straight path in order to make travel more enjoyable. Our turns mustn't be too sharp, nor the hills too steep, lest we find ourselves turned back because our paths have led us to the edges of an abyss. In short, we want to be direct, without being monotonous; funny, without being buffoonish; serious, without being dull. Humor must serve the high purpose of education if it is to have merit. Prior to the first day of my first year, I asked my co-op if I could do an experiment on my students. The purpose of the experiment was to determine the exact level of seriousness necessary to be taken as a first year teacher. I decided to dispense what I had learned from 6 years in college, 4 years as a juvenile court evaluator, and 29 years of life and educate them using only my Phineas and Ferb bag.

A large part of our success as teachers lies in our abilities to maintain the tricky balance that exists between respect for authority and genial overtures made toward our students. To make meaningful jokes and to laugh with students must be couched in respect for the responsibilities inherent to our roles as educators. When humor overwhelms our authority as teachers, we sacrifice the respect that our students should have for us. Just as it is our job to steer our Mayflower through the choppy waters of the educational ocean, keeping our students safe and sound, it is also our job to keep the good ship S.S. Education from hitting the shores of boredom and monotony. We must do this humorously, but with our passengers safe in the knowledge that we are steering this ship in a safe direction. The question then becomes one of how to milk the cow without it laughing.

CHAPTER 25

Incorporating Humor in Different Subjects and Grade Levels

Also, come to understand the nature of the students you are about to teach. Early childhood-aged students often are drawn to slapstick stories. At this age, they enjoy books like Walter the Farting Dog, or The Day My Butt Went Psycho. For students in their hormone-raging years (i.e., middle school), scatological content does best. One teacher noted that mentioning the topic of pickles in passing discussion incidentally captures the same perverse interest. If you can provide punch lines that harness both pickles and farts, you may have melted the neat assemblage of cerebral cells making up a typical middle school student. For kids in high school, humor that includes wrestling and strong language—along with mention of Jason Momoa frequently sends them into convulsions. Engage in what the students find funny but be sure to stay true to your own classroom decorum. A simple understanding that your students come from varying backgrounds allows you as the instructor to know which teaching points are appropriate for their mindsets and which must be shared with your colleagues in the teachers' lounge.

Laughter is an international language and one that greatly enhances interpersonal relationships. College-aged students who perceive a higher level of humor by their teachers in the classroom also indicate they have more satisfaction with that teacher's personal qualities in the classroom.

- Why did the student work at the bakery? She needed Math Dough. - What does the zero say to the Eight? Nice belt! - How is the moon like a dollar? Both have four quarters.

You can use humor in any subject area at any grade level. Mathematics teachers share general math jokes that apply to their course's content area. For Social Studies, Science, and Language Arts, comedic tales often blend the properties of humor with a subject's content. Here are a few math jokes to justify this claim, but the world of humor is expansive:

CHAPTER 26

The Impact of Humor on Academic Performance

A pair of accomplished researchers has summarized the evidence supporting the "wide range of cognitive, affective, and social benefits derived from humor." That powerful analysis of all over five decades of research in the field cataloged the many documented reasons to think of humor not as sour grapes but instead as a kind of wonderful elixir for our students' learning lives. Far from representing a time-wasting distraction or insult to the solemnity of learning, humor can improve students' motivation to engage with class content, reduce their anxiety and worries about that content, and even improve their confidence in their own abilities to master it. And many media have reflected those same results due to a kind of cognitive contagion that spreads when we laugh together, fostering a sense of voluntary connectedness and commonality in our students that can make them more open to the hard, fertile, and necessary discussions, struggles, and risks inherent in the learning process.

To be sure, humor is no panacea. It's not a magic bullet that can bridge gaps between students from widely diverse cultural and linguistic backgrounds, nor is it a one-size-fits-all solution. Not all students enjoy the same kind of humor, and we as educators often need to walk a fine line to ensure that our humor is inclusive of rather than offensive to our students. Yet careful research does suggest that using humor correctly and effectively really does make a difference for our students. Too often we think of humor as something frivolous, as the icing on a cake of serious lecturing or journal-reading that's more appetizing without it. But that view may understate the genuine intellectual benefits of this playful gas.

CHAPTER 27

Strategies for Engaging Shy and Introverted Students through Humor

Introverts are often surrounded by misconceptions. They are not necessarily shy, socially awkward, depressed, or less empathetic than the extroverted population. Instead, they have less need for external stimulation and prefer internal reflection and solitude. Although introverted students may superficially resemble their shy classmates (who are overwhelmed by the impression they are making, considering appropriate transitions, editing their messages, or experiencing negative judgments), introverted students are actually thinking about engagement, generating creativity, and absorbing information before they speak. Avoidance and insistence on lesser interactions with shy or introverted students may reduce not only their active contributions but also their well-being. Regardless of the classes they teach, educators must attempt to engage a spectrum of students, provide examples that promote inclusivity, and ask more thoughtful questions that remain open to diverse personalities.

In discussing the strategies she used to overcome her shyness, educator and speaker Melissa Marotz often shares humorous anecdotes about her transformation from the painfully shy girl she was into the expert speaker she is today. Marotz, Lumen Support Specialist I and adjunct faculty member at Millikin University and Lake Land Community College in Illinois, believes that laughter is universal, opens a portal to learning, facilitates connections, and inspires achievement. Shy students who are engaged in academic humor not only benefit from the content being taught, but may also reduce their anxiety level, improve their relationships, and contribute more to an interactive classroom. Sharing stories helps students find their footing in a classroom. Extroverts hold the power and influence early on in many classrooms, but humor levels the playing field, regardless of students' comfort with language and unfamiliar material.

CHAPTER 28

The Role of Improvisation and Spontaneity in Humorous Teaching

Researchers indicate that scripted teaching often produces excessive stress and job burnout (abbreviated burnout here) and that such negative stressors are not motivating for teachers or students. They argue further that since so many benefits are evident in more spontaneous and improvisational teaching, we should encourage applied research to illuminate how spontaneous, humorous teaching might inculcate more student interest, enhance student academic achievement results, reduce special education referrals and retention rates, and decrease teacher burnout through an increased teacher sense of efficacy. Suggesting increased applied research to validate influential leadership factors is not new, but when one adds humor with the weighty domain of education, the need for increasing such research is obvious. Teacher education programs are currently beset by a nagging external validity issue encumber onerous finances. Nonetheless, the role of improvisation and spontaneity in humorous teaching remains a productive area for administrative and educational research.

One of the reasons so many consider teaching humorous is because the humorous teacher is often more spontaneous and less scripted.

He improvises more in his teaching, showing characteristics similar to those generated while joking with friends, characteristics that often reflect humor in our daily interpersonal relationships. Most college teachers admittedly prefer a planned, organized, and structured course over a disorganized, unplanned, and unstructured one, though they also emphasize the importance of improvisation in great teaching. It is another teacher paradox: What teachers supposedly do naturally daily without fretting in their personal lives (i.e., communicating freely and humorously with friends), they are also supposed to do as easily and frequently in their professional lives without necessarily showing divinely spontaneous genius worthy of an improvisational actor.

CHAPTER 29

Encouraging Collaboration and Teamwork through Humor

Dissection students wrote uproariously about various parts of the body, how we plan to learn the material, and planned their partnerships to collaborate. Understanding of material is enhanced by humor and over the fall, I release the funniest and most helpful iterations anonymously to the class. When I have multiple sections, I often ask permission to share examples with future students. Countless students have admitted to enjoying the assignment so much that equitable partner identification sometimes occurred, utilizing a quick race through the lab portion of the class. A goofy non-bioscientist and doctor who tries to look cold with a cadaver made the prospect less intense for some students.

According to one source, the outcomes for students when humor is done correctly in the classroom are numerous and are achieved easily. While I have at times been accused of overdoing the humor in the classroom, I explain my classroom style by the following statement: "Were the joy I bring to teaching to be described as a side effect, then I am proud of it being the most common side effect in the world." This chapter presents various ways in which methods of humor were utilized in a class setting over multiple departments. In every instance, I establish relevant locality and variety of backgrounds among the students. Questions for further investigation are presented within their corresponding sections.

CHAPTER 30

The Connection between Humor and Emotional Intelligence

As a result of shifting economic conditions over the last decade, team-oriented environments that depend on strong communication skills and creating a positive, inclusive work culture have become particularly important to businesses. In a 2019 white paper authored by Google's research, people analytics, and human resources teams, company researchers set out to discover which human skills were most important in predicting success at Google. The researchers found five top human skills that define the very best managers, and three of these five were closely tied to emotional intelligence. They were putting the well-being, community, and psychological safety of their team first; being approachable and concerned with others' success and well-being; communicating and listening to employees to foster growth; having a clear vision and strategy for the team; and supporting employees to face complex challenges through consistent, transparent, and clear communication.

One of the reasons that humor is so important in interactions is that it can serve as a litmus test of social and emotional intelligence. Many researchers believe that the ability to understand and use humor is connected to a person's overall intelligence. In their review of sixty interdisciplinary papers on humor and emotions, Van Hooff and Crawford concluded that there was solid evidence that theory of mind ability is an important factor in both humor and cinematic appreciation. That is par for the course when it comes to social and emotional intelligence, which have been linked to a variety of success factors and even a person's ability to connect with others on a personal level. Furthermore, recent research suggests that these skill sets have practical applications in the workplace. An increasing number of scholars, practitioners, and companies believe that the potential to outperform in the workplace hinges upon human skills such as emotional intelligence.

CHAPTER 31

Using Humor as a Tool for Classroom Management

As for me, I relied on my humor primarily in creating and maintaining a good rapport with my students. I made sure my comments did not hurt my students, and in most cases, they were aimed at educating them. Although I did not expect to hear it from a student, one such comment was received with the equivalent of applause. I once assessed and graded a test paper of one particular student while he was observing me through a big window at the door of the conference area. Both our classrooms were built in the same wing of the same building. Since it was important for me to maintain my integrity as a teacher as well as to make the boy realize the influence our personal conduct had on our public image, my comment was "..., as much as one should never change his actions simply because he is being watched, ...," said while I was pointing toward him with my free left hand while I was grade-writing the paper with the other.

As a teacher, you, of course, need to guide and control your students – just as smartly and subtly as a good conductor does. The right timing of your comments and warnings is so important. Otherwise, your class might end up like the one that the long-term middle-aged substitute placed across the hall from our room. He had the worst of time keeping the students there in line. I don't know how students tend to sense those weapons that are most sensitive to them through a wall, but they took full advantage of that. The situation got so bad that the teacher found himself standing between the demonstrators at the front of the class and those who had taken the message and were getting ready to leave through the windows at the back of the classroom.

CHAPTER 32

Conclusion

In the final class, which does not really exist, I tell my students to change the priority on which they evaluate things and people in their lives. They will be much happier if they set gaining knowledge, broadening their context, developing their perception, and appreciating art and thinking before, in other words, above, making money. Knowledge has an almost unlimited energy once it is transformed into action, and literally, laughs and loves are the fuels to convert knowledge into relying and workable force, which continuously helps us in our endeavors to reach better goals in our lives. Also, true laughs and loves are more likely to be visited in those who are seeking more knowledge and indulge in expressing caring warmth to others. I end my unfinal class by telling my students that they must be specially good, spectacularly good at exercising the positive force that humor represents, and in profiting this means of expression for their own improvement and in making the world they live ever better for all of us. I want my students to be like Rabelais, the 17th century humorous French character, who continually rejoices about the advances the human race has accomplished in knowledge and culture and makes great fun about those who try to sabotage the path of this advancement. I want my students to be enthusiasts in their variety quests for the intellectual and spiritual achievements for the transforming power of humor as today, the 17th century Rabelais did. I want all of us to keep the 17th century university in high esteem, the discussions, and the writings in which luminaries like Bruno, Galileo, Campanella, Jaucourt, Huygens, Newton, Pascal, Malpighi, Spinoza, just to list a few of the "old" ones, exchanged and developed knowledge, and practiced humor enhancing the standing of our species, Homo Sapiens Habilis throughout the world. I want us, all of us, to keep developing ourselves and our humor while supporting, promoting and directing our conversation towards the enhancement of the human species and the world it lives in. Paraphrasing the late Tim Leary, I thus end up saying to my students and to those of us who are here today: "Turn on, tune in, and be as cool as you think you might become."

Milton Keynes UK
Ingram Content Group UK Ltd.
UKHW040939081224
452111UK00011B/232